W9-AHL-662

T 363.2
P/u
3/04
Q 19.95

CAREERS IN SEARCH AND RESCUE OPERATIONS

CAREERS IN
POLICE DEPARTMENTS'
SEARCH AND RESCUE UNITS

Jennifer Plum

the rosen publishing group's
rosen
central

To my dad,
for while he is not a rescue worker, he has rescued me from many emergencies

Published in 2003 by The Rosen Publishing Group, Inc.
29 East 21st Street, New York, NY 10010

Copyright © 2003 by The Rosen Publishing Group, Inc.

First Edition

All rights reserved. No part of this book may be reproduced in any form without permission in writing from the publisher, except by a reviewer.

Library of Congress Cataloging-in-Publication Data

Plum, Jennifer.
Careers in police departments' search and rescue units/ Jennifer Plum.— 1st ed.
   p. cm. — (Careers in search and rescue operations)
Summary: Discusses the history of search and rescue work by police departments, requirements of becoming a police officer, and the roles various police departments played during and after the events of September 11, 2001. Includes bibliographical references and index.
ISBN 0-8239-3834-4 (library binding)
1. Search and rescue operations—United States—Juvenile literature. 2. Police—Vocational guidance—United States—Juvenile literature. [1. Police—Vocational guidance. 2. Rescue work—Vocational guidance. 3. Vocational guidance.]
I. Title. II. Series.
HV551.3 .P59 2003
363.2'3—dc21

          2002013342

Manufactured in the United States of America

CONTENTS

INTRODUCTION
Serving Communities, Saving Lives

Emergency workers, like police search and rescue workers, protect our communities every day. The tragic events of September 11, 2001, reminded us all how important rescue workers are. While many rushed to leave the World Trade Center, rescue workers rushed in to find and save the people still inside. Among the approximately 3,000 victims were twenty-three New York Police Department members and 343 members of the New York Fire Department.

Police search and rescue workers from around the country packed up their gear and went to New York City to assist in the search for survivors. As people around the world watched the progress on television, emergency workers searched for signs of life in the rubble. Working around the clock, workers exhibited great courage in a time of crisis. When it was clear that there were no survivors, the workers carefully searched for victims' bodies.

How are police search and rescue workers different from other police officers in your community? Teams are trained

Wearing respirators to keep from breathing in harmful dust particles, these police officers carefully probe the wreckage of the World Trade Center on September 29, 2001. Even eighteen days after the terrorist attacks, search and rescue workers had not given up on finding survivors.

specifically to help out in many different emergencies. Some police search and rescue workers have been in the police department for years. Others are trained volunteers who are called in for certain missions.

Police search and rescue workers serve on a variety of missions. Squads work in large urban cities like New York and Chicago, as well as small rural communities. Every day, in any corner of the United States, these workers are doing their job. Some canvass neighborhoods in search of clues for a missing child. Others dangle from a harness on the edges of mountains while assisting stranded rock climbers. Teams of police workers enter unstable buildings and crawl through dark caves. All of this is done to protect and save the lives of others.

Some police search and rescue workers are teamed up with specially trained search dogs, known as K-9s. These special dogs sniff out clues and track down lost individuals. Workers are trained as dog handlers in order to be able to understand their dogs' actions and behavior. Some dogs are even trained to follow a person's smell on the water in the case of a boating accident or drowning.

Some days are rewarding, while other days are long and unglamorous; however, police search and rescue squads work until the job is done. On a successful mission, workers return from the site with an unharmed victim. Other days are spent searching for bodies of the deceased. With enormous amounts of stamina and courage, police rescue squads serve in a unique way.

CHAPTER 1

Key Players in Police Search and Rescue

All police rescue workers have one thing in common—dedication. Each worker fills a vital role. However, no one person can perform the job entirely on his or her own. Teamwork is essential in search and rescue missions. This chapter will discuss the different positions that make up a police search and rescue team.

Police Rescue Technician

Police rescue technicians, or rescue workers, are trained to respond quickly to the public's needs. They are among the first people on-site at a national disaster or natural catastrophe. Rescue technicians risk their lives every day to help strangers who are lost, hurt, trapped, or in danger. Sometimes, it is known that the victim or victims have died. In these cases, police technicians are trained to recover clues about the victim's death as well as the victim's body. This helps the police department determine the cause of death while providing closure to the case.

Search and Rescue Missions: Baby Jessica and the Well

In 1987, eighteen-month-old Jessica McClure was the center of a grueling search and rescue mission outside Midland, Texas. The toddler slipped into an uncovered well twenty-two-feet deep (sixty meters) while playing in her aunt's backyard. The Baby Jessica ordeal captured the attention of millions as people across the United States waited for her rescue. The toddler remained wedged in this space, only eight-inches wide (twenty centimeters), as search and rescue workers toiled above ground. It wasn't until fifty-eight hours later that two paramedics were able to enter the hole they had widened and free Baby Jessica.

Most search and rescue technicians are paid staff members of the police department. Some towns are not large enough for a full-time rescue squad. These areas rely on volunteers and trained law enforcement personnel and firefighters when disaster strikes. Other cities have special squads devoted solely to search and rescue.

Rescue technicians work in teams or units for a police department, public safety department, or emergency services office. Each rescue mission has a team leader or coordinator. This person guides the team and follows a specific search and rescue plan. Similar procedures are followed in most search and rescue cases; however, each mission has unique qualities. These variables are based on the environment, the victim, and specific issues such as the weather. You can read more about creating a rescue plan in chapter 4. Team leaders act as the contact person for all team members, as well as for the families of victims and the media.

When not out saving lives, there is office work to be done. Police rescue workers fill out activity reports and maintain files on missions. Workers also attend regular meetings to stay informed about what is going on in their department. Training sessions help workers keep their skills up-to-date.

K-9

You have probably heard that a dog is a human's best friend. But did you know that dogs save lives, too? Search dogs, or K-9s, are important members of police search and rescue teams. Certain breeds of dogs are great searchers. The most common search dogs are bloodhounds, German shepherds, Labrador retrievers, and some mixed breeds.

Search dogs literally follow their noses and sniff out clues. Each human has an individual scent. This scent is carried by tiny skin cells that fall off the body. The body loses about forty thousand of these skin cells each minute. We lose these cells when we do things as simple as breathing, sweating, or touching things. These cells can travel in the air, in water, and on land, carrying our scent.

A search dog is given an item of clothing with a person's smell on it. The dog then sets out to follow the smell. K-9 dogs can follow a person's scent for long distances. They can often find a scent even days after a person has been in an area. This is helpful in tracking a human through a vast forest or under a lot of rubble. In missing person cases, dogs are brought to various locations to detect whether the person has been in that area.

Because they are small and quick on their feet, K-9s can gain access to areas that can't be reached by humans. They can squeeze into cramped areas created by earthquakes or building damage in order to search for victims. Search dogs must be comfortable riding in trucks, boats, and helicopters. They also must be agile and able to follow directions. Most important, they must be friendly, comfortable around people, and not afraid of strangers. Specific information on necessary training for search dogs can be found in chapter 3.

Ajax, a K-9 search and rescue dog, has traveled all the way from his home in Gordon, Georgia, to Salt Lake City, Utah. His job has brought him to the 2002 Olympic winter games, where he stands guard outside the Medals Plaza.

Did You Know?

Over three hundred K-9 rescue dogs assisted in the search and rescue mission at Ground Zero after the terrorist attacks of September 11, 2001. They came to New York from all over the country, and even from Canada, Puerto Rico, and Europe. This is said to be the largest K-9 rescue effort ever organized.

K-9 Handlers

K-9 handlers, or trainers, work directly with search dogs. Workers know their dogs very well and communicate with them to find missing persons. Handlers know when their dogs are tired or overworked. They also recognize changes in a dog's attitude, which may mean that a dog has detected a clue or scent. Handlers must know a dog's personality and behavior extremely well. They also follow the dog's reactions to changes in wind conditions, temperature, and air patterns.

Ongoing training is important for both dogs and trainers. Trainers should work with the dogs three to four times a week to maintain skills. Training can include following scents of different people. To be prepared for any emergency, it is also a good idea to train in a variety of conditions, such as rainy weather or buildings with lots of hallways and entrances.

Dog handlers are responsible for caring for their dogs. Dogs need food and shelter, as well as training. It can cost up to $3,500 a year to care for a trained K-9. This can be expensive for volunteer K-9 handlers.

Scuba

Sometimes it is not enough to search the surface of the water. Important clues, and a victim's body, may lie far beneath the water. In these situations, teams of police divers are called in. Police divers are trained in rescue diving in open water. They must be familiar with some special techniques. In zero visibility diving, divers must know how to navigate murky and dark waters. Police divers must also be trained in evidence recovery. They must search for evidence and return clues to land for inspection.

Police divers scour for clues on the bottoms of rivers, oceans, and lakes. They search for the remains of missing people under water. They are particularly helpful in recovering a downed aircraft or submerged vehicle.

Volunteer Rescue Workers

Some police search and rescue teams are made up of volunteers who are trained to assist on rescue missions. These volunteers, who provide expertise in a particular area, are not paid for their services. For example, helicopter pilots or experienced rock climbers may assist in special rescues, such as when victims are trapped on high mountains or ledges. Police search and rescue teams may call on volunteers to canvass a specific area during a search for a missing person.

Regular search and rescue volunteers offer more than their time. They are also responsible for maintaining their equipment. They spend time and money ensuring that they are ready to respond to an emergency when called.

Search and Rescue Support

Police search and rescue squads rely on assistance from other agencies and departments for many missions. Some of these other players include the Federal Emergency Management Agency (FEMA), medics, air support, and firefighters.

Medics are trained medical professionals who care for injured victims at a search site. When there are many injured individuals at a disaster site, medics set up triage centers where patients are sorted by severity of injury. At the triage center, it is decided which victims need further care at a hospital or emergency ambulance transportation. Triage centers were set up in New York City on September 11 for those leaving the burning twin towers. Although they were prepared for thousands of victims, most triage centers did not see many patients because so many people died soon after the towers were attacked.

Fire departments and police departments often work closely on rescue missions. For example, trained firefighters are brought

Construction workers were repairing a New York City office building when their scaffolding collapsed. These police and fire department search and rescue workers carefully begin the process of removing one layer of wreckage at a time, looking for victims.

in when dealing with collapsed and damaged buildings, downed aircraft, and damaged electrical wires. These are cases in which fires can easily start and spread quickly.

Air support is sometimes necessary to transport rescue squads and equipment. Helicopters get workers to a search area quicker than if traveling by foot, especially in rocky and mountainous areas. Helicopters give workers an expansive view from above ground, which allows workers to see more clues. They can also evacuate victims quickly when medical help is needed. You can find more information about the use of helicopters in search and rescue missions in chapter 4.

FEMA

The Federal Emergency Management Agency (FEMA) is an independent agency that reports to the president of the United States. FEMA officials are the nation's disaster task force. They respond to disasters, help disaster areas recover, and plan for future disasters. When the president declares an area to be a disaster site, FEMA sends in help. (FEMA also provides support in international disasters.)

FEMA focuses on preparing for disaster. They provide the public with information on preventing injury during natural and manmade disasters. This includes information on how to stay safe during disasters like earthquakes or floods. FEMA also works toward building national security to prevent future terrorist attacks.

CHAPTER 2

Police Search and Rescue Missions

Police search and rescue missions take place in a variety of locations under many different conditions. Teams may work in isolated wilderness environments or in busy cities. One day, a rescue worker may be searching for a missing elderly person. The next day, that technician may search for victims of a rafting accident.

Most missions involve the search and rescue of victims of natural disasters, terrorist activities, or building collapses. Other search and rescue missions involve finding and removing victims from the water, a confined space (like a cave), or high mountain ledges. Some missions involve searching for missing children or adults.

Natural Disasters

A natural disaster is a sudden event in nature that damages natural surroundings and property, and injures people. Examples include floods, hurricanes, earthquakes, winter storms, and volcanic eruptions. Search and rescue workers are called to disaster areas to search for victims and to assist the injured.

Hurricanes

A hurricane is a wild tropical storm with heavy rain and rough ocean waters. Winds must reach speeds over 74 miles (119.1 km) per hour to be classified as a hurricane. Extreme hurricanes may produce winds at a jaw-dropping speed of 160 miles

The historic city of York, England, was hit with massive floods during November of 2000, causing many homes to be evacuated. These policemen use a raft to take a family of four to safety.

(257.5 km) per hour. High winds are dangerous. But for those living near oceans, rough waters resulting from these storms cause even more harm. Ocean waves can reach heights of 20 feet (6 meters). This violent rise in ocean water is known as a storm surge. Such waves can wipe out houses and cause major flooding within minutes.

A hurricane warning is issued when a storm is expected within twenty-four hours. Once a hurricane warning is issued, police evacuate an area and direct citizens to storm shelters. Police squads also search neighborhoods for elderly or physically disabled individuals who may be trapped in their homes. After the hurricane, police workers look for missing people. They also help people who are stranded in damaged buildings or flooded areas.

Floods

According to FEMA, floods are the most common natural disaster. Many communities experience flooding from heavy rain or melting snow. These floods may develop over a few days. More serious flooding occurs when a dam breaks. Dams may be damaged during an earthquake or explosion. Old and poorly designed dams can break easily. Dam failures can cause major destruction When a dam breaks, huge amounts of water are released with no warning.

Flash floods are the most dangerous weather-related hazard. Flash floods usually occur with little or no warning. They occur

Tornadoes

A tornado is a wild and violent windstorm characterized by a funnel-shaped cloud. Tornadoes strike unexpectedly, producing winds as fast as 300 miles (482.8 km) per hour. Violent winds may rip up trees and remove the roofs from homes. A fast-moving tornado may even lift large cars and trucks. Mobile homes are especially at risk for damage from the wild winds.

Emergency workers help people who are trapped in their homes or public buildings. They search for people who have been injured by flying debris during a storm. During a natural disaster like a tornado, family members may get separated from each other. Rescue workers can help lost individuals find their families and give them information on local shelters where they can stay if their homes were damaged.

Winter Storms

Harsh weather can leave people stranded or lost. Extreme snowy and icy conditions are dangerous for skiers or hikers. It is easy to lose your way in blinding snow and wind. Search and rescue missions may take place at large mountains like Mount Rainier in Washington or smaller mountains in New York or in Nevada.

Winter weather rescue missions call for fast work. Survival is difficult in freezing conditions. Search and rescue workers race against the clock to find stranded hikers or lost skiers. Overexposure to the cold can cause frostbite and hypothermia.

Frostbite is a reaction to cold that includes a loss of sensation in the skin. The fingers, toes, nose, and ear lobes are at risk of frostbite. Hypothermia sets in when body temperature drops below 90 degrees Fahrenheit (32.2 degrees Celsius). Symptoms include exhaustion and slowness in speaking or walking. Hypothermia can also cause uncontrollable shivering. Workers must dress appropriately and follow necessary precautions when working in stormy winter blasts. Special clothing includes waterproof jackets and pants to keep workers warm and dry.

Other Situations

- Water search and rescue missions are necessary in situations other than flash floods or hurricanes. Victims of boating accidents or airplane crashes may be missing in lakes, rivers, and oceans. Time is of great importance in water rescue missions. Most people tire easily in the water. Also, hypothermia is a danger for those spending too much time in cold water.

  Police rescue workers specializing in this area must be strong swimmers. They are trained to swim against tides in swift water. Some search and rescue workers are even certified scuba divers and can search for victims underneath the water's surface.

- Some rescue workers may be trained in rescuing individuals from confined spaces. A confined space can be a manhole or a well, for example. Sometimes, a confined space is created when a building collapses and leaves victims stranded in voids underground or underneath piles of rubble. A car can even become a confined space after an accident.

Police search and rescue teams must find out if there are individuals trapped after a natural or man-made disaster. Police rescue workers must identify the location of trapped individuals. It is important for the team to evaluate any dangers or risks. Then they can get to work rescuing the victim. Once freed, the victim may need first aid or emotional assistance.

A specific form of training is required to find people trapped in caves. Some people like to explore caves for fun. But they may get injured inside or lost along the way. A friend or family member may realize that someone they know visited a cave and did not return. Workers must prepare for unique conditions in a cave environment, including darkness and extreme cold. Some cave rescue missions can last up to several days. Rescue workers face the extra challenge of assisting injured victims out of confined spaces.

- High-angle rescue specialists help people who are stuck on high ledges or mountaintops. Victims could include a child in a tree or a window washer trapped on a ledge. In the wilderness, victims include stranded rock climbers or hikers or skiers who have gone off the trail.

Rescue workers must be trained in high-angle rope rescue techniques. Good footwork and confidence is essential, especially in steep, rocky, and muddy terrain. Rescue workers may have to administer first aid while dangling hundreds of feet from the ground. Finally, workers must be able to transport victims to a safe place. Victims are removed with the use of special ropes and carriers, and with collapsible stretchers if possible. This is certainly not a job for anyone afraid of heights.

Missing Persons

Each year, hundreds of police search and rescue missions focus on missing persons in towns and cities around the United States. The Federal Bureau of Investigation (FBI) notes that there were 876,213 missing persons reported in 2000. Typically, 85 to 90 percent of these missing individuals are children under the age of eighteen.

Missing adults and children come from a variety of backgrounds. Missing children may be separated from their parents or guardians or they simply become lost. This can happen at the mall, a family picnic, or at an amusement park, for example. Sometimes, children go missing because they have been abducted or kidnapped by strangers, family members, or friends. Also, thousands of children run away each year and leave few clues behind.

Adults may go missing for a variety of reasons. Elderly individuals and people suffering from memory loss may wander away from their homes and disappear. Adults with mental illnesses may also leave their families or homes and be missing for days before they are tracked down. Some adults run away in the same way that children might, and leave behind few clues about where they have gone.

Police search and rescue workers collect clues about the missing person before they begin a search. They talk to family

This K-9 search and rescue dog is on the trail of a fourteen-year-old girl who was kidnapped from her home. Starting with the area around the girl's home, the rescue crew searches for a clue that might help lead to her whereabouts.

members and friends and ask questions about the victim. They need to figure out whether the person was abducted or whether he or she might have run away. They also need to know about the missing person's mental and physical conditions. They question witnesses who saw the missing person before he or she disappeared.

Once police teams have started finding answers to these questions, they can search specific areas where the individual was last seen. Trained dogs assist police search and rescue teams by tracing the smell of the missing person. Police departments work with other agencies and police squads from other cities or states to trace the path of the missing person. They can also release information to the public so that everyone can be on the lookout for the missing person.

Terrorism

Terrorism is the use of violence to intimidate people. Terrorist acts may occur within the United States because of domestic groups or international organizations. An example of a terrorist organization is Al Qaeda, the group responsible for the terrorist attacks in the United States on September 11, 2001.

In the event of terrorist activity, search and rescue workers must be prepared to work under grueling and emotionally difficult situations. Terrorism is not limited to bombing attacks. It can also involve attacks on a water supply or on

Did You Know?

Harrison Ford is not only a famous actor but also a hero. Ford lends his expertise as a trained pilot as well as the use of his private helicopter to assist local police departments and national parks on search and rescue missions for lost hikers. He rescued a lost hiker in the mountains of Wyoming in July 2000 and a lost Boy Scout from Yellowstone National Park in July 2001.

public transportation. In Tokyo, Japan, nerve gas was released into the subway system by a cult organization in 1995. This attack killed twelve people and injured 5,300 more during a busy rush hour. The government and police forces fear the use of chemical or biological weapons by terrorists in the United States. Search and rescue teams must be prepared to respond to terrorist actions with no warning.

CHAPTER 3

Responsibilities and Risks

All police search and rescue workers must have certain characteristics, like courage and perseverance. Other skills must be learned. Training helps workers complete their jobs successfully and deal with the physical and emotional risks common to rescue work. In this chapter, you will learn about the training and skills necessary to work on a police search and rescue squad.

Do You Have What It Takes?

Search and rescue workers must be confident and mature. Workers often must make quick decisions on the job, which may be a matter of life or death. Workers deal with stressful conditions and must be able to stay calm during a disaster. Finally, excellent health and stamina are necessary to work on long and physically challenging missions.

Do you know any survival skills? Can you build a fire or make shelter out of limited materials? Most important, can you

Historical Search and Rescue Missions: Ground Zero—The World Trade Center

The attacks of September 11, 2001, were the most devastating terrorist attacks on U.S. soil. Hoping to find survivors, rescue units worked through twelve-hour shifts at Ground Zero. Police rescue squads from all over the United States worked side by side with other volunteer teams, such as the New York Fire Department and the New York Police Department. On September 30, 2001, the mission was officially changed from a rescue mission to a recovery effort. The goal of the recovery effort was to find remains of victims and to clear out debris using cranes and heavy equipment.

keep your cool? All search and rescue workers must be familiar with survival techniques and strategies. What kind of tools would you need if you were stranded in the wilderness? If your answer included a map and compass, you are correct. But do you know how to use these tools?

Search and rescue workers must read and understand maps. They should recognize symbols and understand concepts such as longitude and latitude. Rescue workers may find themselves relying on a compass to navigate the wilderness. It is important to follow directions when using a compass. It is equally important to be able to give others directions based on a compass reading.

Finally, are you a people person? Do you enjoy interacting with others or do you prefer to work on projects alone? Police search and rescue workers must enjoy working with others. Squad leaders need good communication skills in order to give directions to teams and interact with other agencies and the families of the victims. Good people skills are also necessary for assisting the injured or missing when they are found. Workers offer support to people who may have experienced something traumatic.

Training

Search and rescue workers must be trained in first aid, cardio-pulmonary resuscitation (CPR), wilderness survival skills, and knot-tying skills. Specialized rescue workers, such as high-angle rescue specialists, receive specific training for their areas. Rescue workers must be certified in search and rescue techniques, as well as first aid. Some squads may require workers to first receive training as emergency medical technicians to master these skills.

National Association of Search and Rescue (NASAR)

The National Association of Search and Rescue (NASAR) is an organization that offers training in search and rescue tactics. NASAR offers search and rescue technicians a test and guidelines on training. Most police departments require workers to pass the NASAR test before they work on a rescue squad. The exam is made up of 160 questions. It tests knowledge of search and rescue techniques, map and compass skills, and rope skills. An understanding of search philosophy and techniques is needed to pass the test.

In addition to the written exam, there are practical exam exercises. This gives applicants a chance to show off their skills. These exercises evaluate skills in:

- Reading and understanding maps

- Identifying and tracking footprints

- Packing the necessary equipment

- Tying basic knots

- Locating and labeling clues

- Following routine search tactics

K-9 Training

K-9 dogs undergo intense training before they work on emergency cases. Each K-9 is trained in a specialty, such as tracking, trailing, or air scent. A tracking dog is trained to follow a subject's scent in the air. These dogs trace the victim's exact footsteps. A trailing dog is also trained to pick up the subject's smell in an area, but the technique is slightly different. Trailing dogs work on a shorter leash and they use the wind to follow the subject's smell. Air-scent dogs are trained to work without a leash. These dogs are exposed to a subject's scent, then they take off on their own to find the smell.

When the dog finds a clue or scent, he or she is trained to let the handler know by giving a sign, known as an alert. An alert can be a bark or a change in the position of the dog's ears or tail. It is important to reward the dog during the search. A reward may be a favorite toy or game, for example.

Once dogs receive their training, they may work in a specific area. While some dogs are trained to follow a scent in the air, others work in the water. Some K-9s focus on urban rescue missions and navigate unstable buildings. Others specialize in cadaver searches. These dogs search for lost persons who are thought to have died. After death, a body gives off particular scents as it decomposes. Cadaver dogs are familiar with these smells and can lead rescue workers to a body.

Some dogs go through rigorous training for FEMA. These dogs must pass a series of tests. Tasks include climbing ladders, walking on planks 6 feet (1.8 meters) above ground, and navigating unsteady terrain. It generally takes two years to train dogs for this test.

Training is ongoing for all search and rescue workers and canines. Most squads offer mandatory training sessions regularly in order to maintain skills. Simulated rescue drills help dogs and workers stay prepared for when real disaster strikes.

Because K-9s can sniff out hidden bomb materials, they are often used for security purposes. This Secret Service agent and his K-9 companion carefully examine a truck before it enters the White House gates.

Risks

Of course, there are many risks involved for workers in police search and rescue departments. These include not only the more obvious physical dangers, but also emotional risks as well. Rescue work can be stressful, and workers must be prepared to deal with this stress.

Physical Risks

Police search and rescue workers face physical dangers every day. Some risks are associated with the environment and the weather. Altitude sickness is a threat to workers on high mountains. Altitude sickness occurs when a person's body cannot function properly at a higher altitude. Symptoms include tiredness and a feeling of weakness.

Police rescue workers must take all the necessary precautions to protect themselves. It is important to be in good physical shape and to be well rested. Sometimes, police and rescue workers work long and irregular schedules. Workers must get enough sleep to stay alert on the job.

Workers should always wear protective gear, like helmets when rafting or biking and lifejackets when on the water. Workers should not perform tasks that they are not trained for, like rock climbing or fire rescue. Workers must know their personal limits and stick to them.

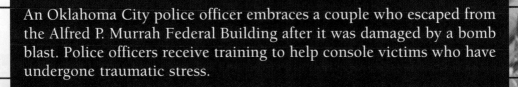

An Oklahoma City police officer embraces a couple who escaped from the Alfred P. Murrah Federal Building after it was damaged by a bomb blast. Police officers receive training to help console victims who have undergone traumatic stress.

Emotional Risks

Almost everyone faces some stress at work—from preschool teachers to bankers. As mentioned, rescue workers typically work under enormous pressure and stress. Overwhelming stress can lead to emotional problems.

Rescue workers face danger, injury, and death every day. Rescue workers must also deal with the potential loss of their coworkers on the job. They are involved on a personal level with missions and tragedies that affect their communities.

Some rescue workers deal with depression or other emotional problems when a mission ends. While media attention acknowledges heroic acts, it also puts pressure on workers to always succeed. Workers may feel anger, grief, or shock while a mission is going on or after it has finished. These feelings can put a strain on relationships and cause emotional problems. Post-traumatic stress disorder is a common condition many workers experience after being involved in a rescue mission such as the World Trade Center or Oklahoma City bombing.

How can workers protect themselves from emotional distress? For one thing, it is important to communicate with coworkers who share a common experience. Talking about feelings of sadness or depression can be helpful. Squad leaders may offer debriefing sessions when a mission is completed so that workers can talk about their experiences and share feelings. Workers should also stay close with family and friends. Spending time with loved ones can help workers get through stressful times.

CHAPTER 4

Operations and Equipment

Solid planning and organization is key to every search and rescue mission. Each mission must have a clear search strategy or plan. Workers must also know how to operate equipment and use timesaving technology.

Developing a Search Strategy

Every search strategy is unique. Plans vary greatly depending on the specific circumstances of a mission. Every aspect of the mission must be considered before a plan can be created. The first step in creating a strategy is to collect clues and hints. One important task is identifying the place where a missing person was last seen. This is known as the point last seen, or PLS. PLS gives a search and rescue team an idea of where to begin its search. PLS is especially helpful when searching for a child who has wandered off or disappeared. PLS also helps to guide the team in cases involving lost hikers or overboard fishers.

Search and Rescue Missions: Oklahoma City Bombing

On April 19, 1995, a bomb that exploded outside the Alfred P. Murrah Federal Building in Oklahoma City, Oklahoma, killed 168 people. Police rescue workers, firefighters, federal workers, and civilians searched for survivors in the rubble of the building. Approximately twelve hundred police rescue workers, as well as rescue dogs, searched for survivors and recovered bodies. Even cave-rescue specialists were called in to save victims trapped under piles of concrete. Rescue workers found the last survivor fourteen hours after the explosion.

Using this information, the search area can be defined. Workers evaluate natural boundaries as well as how quickly the victim could be moving, if at all. It is helpful to define the probability of area, or POA. This further confines a search area and focuses the rescue mission. Police may block exits from a search area to prevent the victim, or any criminals, from leaving the area. Guards can be posted around the perimeter or roadblocks can be set up nearby.

Once the search area is identified, police rescue leaders must decide how to proceed. Is the area safe? Are buildings unstable and not fit for entry? How will changes in weather affect the mission? Are there special conditions that police workers should be prepared for? Answering these and other questions is necessary for a safe plan. Squad leaders must think of not only a quick rescue or recovery, but also workers' safety.

At the beginning of the search, it is important to consider the nature of the mission. Has the victim disappeared or been injured voluntarily? Is foul play or criminal activity involved? If it is a criminal case, police must contain the search area and collect clues to find the victim and the criminal.

Man Tracking

Man tracking allows searchers to gather clues and follow a subject's path. Training in man tracking teaches rescue workers how to read their surroundings and interpret every clue. Signs as obvious as a footprint or as delicate as displaced soil can lead searchers in the right direction. Rescuers also look for damaged plants or grass or moved rocks or pebbles scattered on a foot-path. Sometimes, a victim may leave behind a gum wrapper, used tissue, or personal items. These are all signs that someone has passed through an area.

Man tracking can be extremely helpful in unpopulated or isolated areas. This makes it an effective strategy in the wilderness.

BEATRICE PUBLIC LIBRARY
BEATRICE, NE 68310

However, it is not as effective in popular areas, such as a well-traveled trail in Yosemite National Park or a busy street in Atlanta, Georgia. In the right environment, however, careful searching can lead to strong clues. But be warned—some clues can point to an animal, like a deer or rabbit, passing through the area.

Washington police officers scour the ground for clues while investigating a missing persons case in Rock Creek Park, Washington, D.C.

Search and Rescue Equipment

Each search and rescue mission requires special equipment. Large equipment, including cranes and bulldozers, clears out heavy debris from collapsed buildings or roads. This may be the first step or the last step in a mission, depending on the stability of a disaster site. Sometimes, workers rely on their own hands and buckets to slowly and carefully clear out debris. Cranes and hydraulic lifts bring workers to various floors of a damaged building to search for survivors. This way, workers are able to look for trapped victims in an unstable building while keeping a safe distance.

Police rescue workers must carry personal rescue equipment. Communication tools such as radios and pagers are essential. Special clothing, such as protective rain gear and winter weather coats, is vital. Other helpful items include a flashlight, helmet, knife, headlamp, batteries, whistle, compass, and matches. Necessary food and water must be packed for longer trips. If rescue workers do not take care of themselves, how can they help others?

Search and rescue dogs also have special equipment. Most dogs wear a special vest for missions. Many also wear a bell around their necks so that they can be heard as they move through a search area. When searching at night, dogs may wear a special light so that they can see ahead of them and be seen in the dark. Also, rescue vehicles should always be stocked with the right equipment. Ropes, pulleys, harnesses, and other rock-climbing materials are frequently used items, as are boards and equipment to transport victims. Radios and wireless communication equipment is needed to keep workers connected. Medical equipment should always be available, including general first-aid kits, airway packs, and splints.

Some rescue missions require special vehicles. Police workers use motorcycles or all-terrain vehicles (ATVs) in rugged terrain. Mountain bikes can be helpful to navigate narrow, rocky trails or crowded city streets. Snowmobiles and skis are often the best form of transportation in the snow. Boats allow access to smaller islands and are necessary in water rescues. Sometimes, horses are used to get through parks and woods quickly.

Helicopters

Workers rely on helicopters in a variety of missions. However, they are expensive to purchase and maintain. Therefore, many police teams are unable to afford their own helicopters. Instead, they rely on local television stations, private businesses, and even the armed services for helicopter use when necessary.

Anyone riding in a helicopter must be trained in aircraft safety. It is important for all rescue workers to know when it is safe to approach a helicopter as it is landing. Approaching or exiting a helicopter at the wrong time can lead to injury. Rescue dogs are trained to safely board and unload from a helicopter.

Because helicopters offer search and rescue workers a great view of a search area, it is often easier to notice clues below. Searchers may notice clues such as ski tracks, a tent, or a downed airplane more quickly from the sky. Helicopters also provide access to areas that are difficult to reach by foot, such as canyons and cliffs. Finally, a helicopter flying overhead may attract the subject's attention.

The 1996 crash of ValuJet Flight 592 left wreckage strewn over a large area of the Florida Everglades. Pictured here, rescue workers search through the debris, looking for survivors.

Helicopters serve another important purpose in search and rescue missions—they transport workers and bulky equipment. This is especially helpful when the search area is mountainous or difficult to navigate on foot. If necessary, helicopters can transport any injured victims to a local hospital.

Search and Rescue Technology

Technology simplifies people's jobs every day. This is also true in police search and rescue occupations. Thanks to advanced technology, police teams accomplish many tasks that were once thought impossible.

Technology aids workers who are looking for victims trapped beneath the rubble of damaged highways or buildings. Thermal sensors detect body heat under vast piles of wreckage. In addition to saving time, this technology guides rescue workers to survivors. Special listening devices can be used to detect a victim's breathing under debris. Tiny fiber-optic cameras can be attached to long poles in order to view pictures of areas that are unreachable. Robots have been created that can search for victims in dangerous and unstable buildings and areas. And this is only the beginning— search and rescue workers use technology in many different forms.

Global Positioning System

Can you imagine using a computer to track down a friend's exact location in your city? There is technology that can help you do

Did You Know?

Many people rely on wireless technology for communication on a daily basis. Wireless technology provider Motorola, Inc., recently equipped several police rescue squads in Pinellas County, Florida, with wireless videoconferencing tools. Search vehicles now have a color, touch-screen panel that can receive live video streams. These allow rescue workers to view information about victims and even get information about natural disasters or other catastrophes as they occur. They also let rescue workers see important information such as floor plans and emergency exits for an unstable building. All of this information is extremely helpful when creating a rescue plan.

exactly that. Global positioning system (GPS) technology allows users to quickly identify an exact position anywhere in the world. Global positioning systems use satellites to measure a precise location on earth. Rescue workers carry a small unit that reads transmissions from these special satellites. These units are often as tiny as a small calculator.

GPS technology helps search and rescue teams be able to clearly identify their location in a search area. This is helpful if a team member becomes lost or has to call in for more assistance on how to get to a specific site. GPS simplifies a rescue worker's job. However, GPS technology can be expensive, and not all police departments have access to it.

Emergency Locator Transmitter (ELT)

You may have heard of the black box mentioned during the search after a plane crash. This black box is an emergency locator transmitter, or ELT. Most private aircraft and boats carry an ELT that allows officials to locate a plane or boat in an emergency. In the event of a crash, explosion, or other damage to the aircraft or boat, the ELT emits noises that lead searchers to the site. Police search and rescue workers are trained to monitor and trace the sounds from these devices. This can help rescue workers find a downed airplane or helicopter or a lost boat more quickly.

Although it is not widely used, a similar device has been created for personal use. Known as a personal locator beacon, or PLB, it operates as a black box for an individual. The PLB is activated manually by a person who is lost or in danger. PLBs are not widely used in the United States. However, the technology can protect individuals working in remote and even dangerous locations. Some residents in Oregon and Alaska are helping to field test PLBs.

The Internet

The Internet allows for the quick and simple transfer of information using computers. Some police search and rescue squads find the Internet helpful in certain cases, especially when missing persons are involved. In such cases, police departments can access national crime databases to find out about similar abductions or kidnappings in the area. This may help a rescue squad in developing a search strategy.

The Internet invites the public to help in some search and rescue missions. Information about missing children or adults can be posted on Web sites, including pictures and details about a victim. This keeps the public informed and makes them part of the extended search team. Citizens inform the police if they have any information on a missing person.

The Internet is also a helpful preventive tool. Hikers and rock climbers can check weather conditions before heading to a national park. Skiers can follow large storms on the Internet before beginning a cross-country ski adventure. Boaters can trace the path of tropical storms or hurricanes. People can also get information on natural disasters to feel well-prepared in the event of an emergency. FEMA offers information on topics including earthquakes, tornadoes, and terrorism. Knowing how to handle an emergency can decrease the number of injuries and necessary search and rescue missions, and can also help workers do their jobs.

GLOSSARY

abduct The act of taking a person against his or her will, as in a kidnapping.

air-scent dog A specially trained K-9 dog that follows a subject's scent while not working on a leash.

air support Teams of workers in helicopters and other aircraft used to transport rescue squads and equipment and search for missing persons during a search and rescue mission.

alert A sign from a K-9 or rescue dog given to the handler when the dog finds a clue or scent.

altitude sickness A condition that occurs when a person's body cannot function properly at a high altitude—often includes symptoms of tiredness and weakness.

cadaver dog A K-9 dog trained to find bodies of the deceased based on smell.

emergency locator transmitter (ELT) A technological device carried by aircraft and boats that emits noises in case of an accident to lead rescue workers to the site of the wreckage.

evidence recovery The process in police scuba search and rescue work of searching for clues underwater and bringing them back to the water's surface.

Federal Emergency Management Agency (FEMA) An independent agency that acts as the nation's disaster task force, working to respond to disaster, help disaster areas recover, and prevent future disasters.

flash flood A dangerous flood that produces fast-moving water with little or no warning during an intense rain storm.

frostbite A reaction to extreme cold that produces a loss of sensation in the skin, especially the fingers, toes, nose, and ear lobes.

global positioning system (GPS) Technology that uses satellites and handheld devices to measure a person's precise location anywhere in the world.

high-angle rescues Rescue missions that take place at high angles, such as steep mountainsides or building tops, using special ropes and rock-climbing equipment.

hypothermia A condition that occurs when body temperature drops below 90 degrees Fahrenheit (32.2 degrees Celsius), characterized by exhaustion, slowness of speech, and uncontrollable shivering.

K-9 Rescue dogs specially trained to assist police search and rescue teams with collecting clues and searching for missing people by scent.

K-9 handler A trained individual who works with rescue dogs to find clues and missing persons on a police search and rescue team.

man tracking Procedures that allow searchers to gather clues about a missing person and follow a subject's path by watching for clues, such as moved soil, footprints, or items left behind by the subject.

medic A trained medical professional who cares for injured victims at a search and rescue site.

National Association of Search and Rescue (NASAR) A national search and rescue organization that offers training and certification in search and rescue techniques.

personal locator beacon (PLB) A technological device, which gives off noises, that can be manually operated by an individual in the event of an accident or injury in an isolated area.

point last seen (PLS) The place where a missing person was last seen by witnesses; this helps rescue teams to create a search strategy.

police rescue technician Police worker trained to work on search and rescue missions in a variety of settings and locations.

post-traumatic stress disorder A condition faced by some police search and rescue workers after completing a stressful mission, characterized by feelings of depression, overwhelming stress, and sadness.

probability of area (POA) The confined search area based on how far the victim may have traveled over time.

search strategy A plan that is created for each search and rescue mission to find and save as many victims as possible in a short amount of time.

storm surge A violent rise in ocean water that creates a dome of waves reaching up to 20 feet (6 meters).

terrorism The use of violence to intimidate.

thermal sensor Technological equipment that detects body heat under piles of wreckage to locate survivors of a building collapse or to find missing persons.

tracking dog A K-9 dog trained to follow a subject's exact trail by finding the person's scent in the air.

trailing dog A K-9 dog trained to pick up a subject's scent. The dog does this by following a winding path and tracing the subject's scent in the wind.

triage center An area set up at a disaster site or an emergency location where victims receive medical attention.

volunteer rescue workers Unpaid search and rescue workers who assist on police squads during specific rescue missions.

zero visibility diving A special form of scuba diving that involves navigating dark and murky waters in which divers are unable to see clearly.

FOR MORE INFORMATION

In the United States

International Rescue and Emergency Care Association (IRECA)
P.O. Box 13527
Charleston, SC 29422-3527
(800) 221-3435
Web site: http://www.ireca.org

Mountain Rescue Association
P.O. Box 501
Poway, CA 92074-0501
Web site: http://www.mra.org

National Association for Search and Rescue (NASAR)
4500 Southgate Place, Suite 100
Chantilly, VA 20151-1714
(703) 222-6277
Web site: http://www.nasar.org

North American Police Work Dog Association
4222 Manchester Avenue
Perry, OH 44081
(888) 422-6463
Web site: http://www.napwda.com

Rescue 3 International
9075 Elk Grove Boulevard, #200
P.O. Box 519
Elk Grove, CA 95759-0519
(916) 685-3066
Web site: http://www.rescue3.com

United States Police Canine Association
P.O. Box 80
Springboro, OH 45066
(800) 531-1614
Web site: http://www.uspcak9.com

In Canada

National Search and Rescue Secretariat
400-275 Slater Street
Ottawa, ON K1A 0K2
(800) 727-9414
Web site: http://www.nss.gc.ca

Search and Rescue Society of British Columbia
P.O. Box 1146
Victoria, BC V8W 2T6
(250) 384-6696
Web site: http://www.sarbc.org

Web Sites

Due to the changing nature of Internet links, the Rosen Publishing Group, Inc., has developed an online list of Web sites related to the subject of this book. This site is updated regularly. Please use this link to access the list:

http://www.rosenlinks.com/csro/pdsr/

FOR FURTHER READING

Bulanda, Susan. *Ready to Serve, Ready to Save: Strategies of Real-Life Search and Rescue Missions.* Sun City, AZ: Doral Publishing, 1999.

Bulanda, Susan, and Luana Luther, ed. *Ready! The Training of the Search and Rescue Dog.* Sun City, AZ: Doral Publishing, 1995.

Gerritsen, Resi, and Ruud Haak. *K-9 Search and Rescue.* Calgary, AB: Detselig Enterprises/Termeron Books, 1999.

Giacobello, John. *Scuba Divers: Life Under Water* (Extreme Careers). New York: The Rosen Publishing Group, Inc., 2001.

Hill, Kenneth. *Managing the Lost Person Incident* (MLPI). Chantilly, VA: NASAR, 1997.

Johnson, Glen. *Tracking Dog: Theory and Methods.* Mechanicsberg, PA: Barkleigh Productions, Inc., 1999.

Life Magazine Staff. *One Nation: America Remembers September 11, 2001.* New York: Little, Brown & Company, 2001.

National Association of Search and Rescue. *Introduction to Search and Rescue.* Chantilly, VA: NASAR, 1999.

BIBLIOGRAPHY

Beartooth Search Dogs. "About Wilderness Search Dogs."
    Retrieved June 1, 2002 (http://montanasearchdogs.com/
    faq/about_search_dogs.htm).

Beck, Melinda. "Get Me Out of Here." *Newsweek*, Vol. 125,
    No. 18, May 1, 1995, pp. 40–46.

Brown, Chip. "'Baby Jessica: 5 Years Later." *Houston Chronicle*,
    October 11, 1992.

Brown, Heidi Nolte. "Rubble Rovers to the Rescue in
    Disaster." *Los Angeles Times*, November 16, 1989.

Carney, Steve. "It's All for the Worst; Rescue Teams Join Forces
    in Disaster Drill to Hone Skills." *Los Angeles Times*, January
    29, 1998.

CNN.com/SCI-TECH. "Florida Police, Rescue Squads Test
    Wireless Technology." Retrieved May 29, 2002 (http://www.
    cnn.com/2001/TECH/internet/08/09/police.wireless.idg).

Federal Emergency Management Agency. "Backgrounder: Earthquakes." Retrieved March 30, 2002 (http://www.fema.gov/hazards/earthquakes/quakef.shtm).

Federal Emergency Management Agency. "Backgrounder: Floods and Flash Floods." Retrieved March 5, 2002 (http://www.fema.gov/hazards/floods/flood.shtm).

Federal Emergency Management Agency. "Backgrounder: Terrorism." Retrieved March 30, 2002 (http://www.fema.gov/hazards/terrorism/terrorf.shtm).

Federal Emergency Management Agency. "Backgrounder: Tornadoes." Retrieved March 5, 2002 (http://www.fema.org/hazards/tornadoes/tornado.shtm).

Guy, Andrew, Jr. "A Dog's Duty: Canines Trained to Give Humans a Helping Hand." *Houston Chronicle*, October 16, 2001.

Hill, Kenneth A., and Donald C. Bower. "GPS Navigation in Land Search." Retrieved May 30, 2002 (http://www.sarinfo.bc.ca/Gpssarnav.htm).

Katz, Jesse. "After Baby Jessica, No One Could Rescue the Rescuer." *Houston Chronicle*, May 28, 1985.

Las Vegas Metropolitan Police Department Search and Rescue. "ELT Training." Retrieved March 5, 2002 (http://www.lvmpdsar.com/elttx.html).

Las Vegas Metropolitan Police Department Search and Rescue. "Search and Rescue Officers." Retrieved March 5, 2002 (http://www.lvmpdsar.com/officers.html).

Las Vegas Metropolitan Police Department Search and Rescue. "Unit Equipment." Retrieved March 5, 2002 (http://www.lvmpdsar.com/equip.html).

Las Vegas Metropolitan Police Department Search and Rescue. "Unit Training." Retrieved March 5, 2002 (http://www.lvmpdsar.com/train.html).

Life Magazine Staff. *One Nation: America Remembers September 11, 2001*. New York: Little Brown & Company, 2001.

National Center for Post-Traumatic Stress Disorder. "Disaster Rescue and Response Workers." Retrieved April 30, 2002 (http://www.ncptsd.org/facts/disasters/fs_rescue_workers.html.

Ohio Valley Search and Rescue, Inc. "Vocabulary." Retrieved April 30, 2002 (http://www.vwsar.org/vocab.html).

Rescue 3 International. "Swiftwater Rescue Fact Sheet." Retrieved May 7, 2002 (http://www.rescue3.com/articles09.html).

Reynolds, Christopher. "Much Talk, Little Action on Charging for Rescues." *Los Angeles Times*, December 20, 1998.

Search and Rescue Information. "Search Techniques." Retrieved May 30, 2002 (http://www.sarinfo.bc.ca/Techniqs.htm).

Search and Rescue Society of British Columbia. "The 5 Stages of Search and Rescue." Retrieved April 30, 2002 (http://www.sarbc.org/stages/html).

INDEX

About the Author

Jennifer Plum is a freelance writer who works in educational publishing in Baltimore, Maryland. She is currently working toward her M.F.A. in creative nonfiction at Goucher College.

Photo Credits

Cover © Gene Shaw/TimePix; p. 1 © Jeff Haynes/Corbis; p. 5 © Elise Amendola/AP/Wide World Photos; p. 8 © Bruno Torres/Corbis; p. 11 © Amy Sacetta/AP/Wide World Photos; p. 15 © Corbis; p. 18 © Dan Chung/Corbis; p. 26 © Steve C. Wilson/AP/Wide World Photos; p. 30 © Beth A. Keiser/AP/Wide World Photos; p. 34 © Evan Vucci/AP/Wide World Photos; p. 36 © Pat Carter/AP/Wide World Photos; p. 41 © Stephen J. Boitano/AP/Wide World Photos; p. 44 © Rick Bowmer/AP/Wide World Photos.

Editor

Annie Sommers

Designer

Nelson Sá